Masters of Music

THE WORLD'S GREATEST COMPOSERS

The Life and Times of

Franz Liszt

Mitchell Lane
PUBLISHERS

P.O. Box 196
Hockessin, Delaware 19707

Masters of Music

THE WORLD'S GREATEST COMPOSERS

Titles in the Series
The Life and Times of...

Visit us on the web: www.mitchelllane.com

Comments? email us: mitchelllane@mitchelllane.com

Masters of Music
THE WORLD'S GREATEST COMPOSERS

The Life and Times of

Franz Liszt

by Jim Whiting

Printing   2   3   4   5   6   7   8
    Library of Congress Cataloging-in-Publication Data
Whiting, Jim, 1943-
    The life and times of Franz Liszt/Jim Whiting.
         p. cm. — (Masters of Music)
    Includes bibliographical references (p.) and index.
    ISBN 1-58415-280-X (lib bdg.)
    1. Liszt, Franz. 1811-1886. 2. Composers—Biography—Juvenile literature. I. Title. II. Series.
    ML3930.L57W55   2004
    780'.92—dc22   2004002058
    ISBN 13: 9781584152804

ABOUT THE AUTHOR: Jim Whiting has been a journalist, writer, editor, and photographer for more than 20 years. In addition to a lengthy stint as publisher of *Northwest Runner* magazine, Mr. Whiting has contributed articles to the *Seattle Times, Conde Nast Traveler, Newsday,* and *Saturday Evening Post.* He has edited more than 20 titles in the Mitchell Lane Real-Life Reader Biography series and Unlocking the Secrets of Science. He lives in Washington state with his wife and two teenage sons.

PHOTO CREDITS: Cover: PhotoResearchers; p. 1 SuperStock; p. 3 SuperStock; p. 6 SuperStock; p. 11 Getty Images; p. 14 PhotoResearchers; p. 18 Corbis; p. 19 SuperStock; p. 22 PhotoResearchers; p. 25 PhotoResearchers; p. 27 SuperStock; p. 30 PhotoResearchers; p. 35 Getty Images; p. 36 PhotoResearchers; p. 39 Corbis; p. 40 SuperStock; p. 43 Barbara Marvis.

PUBLISHER'S NOTE: This story is based on the author's extensive research, which he believes to be accurate. Documentation of such research is contained on page 47.

    The internet sites referenced herein were active as of the publication date. Due to the fleeting nature of some web sites, we cannot guarantee they will all be active when you are reading this book.

Contents

The Life and Times of
Franz Liszt

by Jim Whiting

* For Your Information

The Beatles as they appeared at the height of their fame during the 1960s. From left, they are Ringo Starr (whose real name was Richard Starkey), Paul McCartney, George Harrison and John Lennon. Their appearance on The Ed Sullivan Show in 1964 attracted one of the largest audiences in television history.

CHAPTER I

Lisztomania

The most important event in the history of rock music in the United States took place on the evening of February 9, 1964. An estimated 73 million Americans gathered around their television sets, which at that time showed programs mostly in black and white. They were watching *The Ed Sullivan Show*, an entertainment variety program on the CBS network.

For many people, watching *The Ed Sullivan Show* was a regular Sunday-evening ritual. But it had never attracted so many viewers. It had also never had such a demand for studio-audience tickets. More than 50,000 people had tried to get them. But there was room for only 703. The lucky ones—almost all of them teenage girls—sat on the edge of their seats.

They were there to watch the American debut of a band that was already wildly popular in England. It consisted of four young men from the seaport city of Liverpool. Their names were George Harrison, John Lennon, Paul McCartney, and Ringo Starr. They were the Beatles, and as journalist Sandy Gardiner wrote the previous year, "A new disease is sweeping through Britain, Europe and the Far East . . . and doctors are powerless to stop it."[1]

Gardiner called this "disease" Beatlemania. People became so carried away by their intense emotions that they would do things they probably never would have thought of doing otherwise.

It was obvious that Beatlemania had crossed the Atlantic on that memorable evening. As soon as Ed Sullivan introduced the band and they began playing "All My Loving," the girls in the audience began screaming and crying. The wave of emotion continued as John, Paul, George, and Ringo played four more songs: "Till There Was You," "She Loves You," "I Saw Her Standing There," and "I Want To Hold Your Hand." Their performance may have even provided a brief cure for illegal activity. According to reports, the crime rate in major U.S. cities dropped dramatically during the time the show was being broadcast.

That was just the beginning. The Beatles appeared several more times on *The Ed Sullivan Show* in the following months, and they also performed a number of live concerts. The way people reacted was perfectly depicted the following year when Beatlemania led to box-office magic as millions of moviegoers thronged to see *A Hard Day's Night.* Told in a sort of documentary style, the film opens with George, John, Paul, and Ringo being chased by a mob of several hundred teenage girls. The members of the mob don't mean any harm. They just want to get as close as possible to their idols, maybe even touch them or grab a piece of clothing as a souvenir. The four young men try to shake their pursuers. But they can't. Finally they jump on a train just as it is pulling out of a station and escape. The rest of the film shows them preparing for a concert and then performing it.

"Women in the audience screamed and fought for a souvenir— half of a handkerchief, a few strands of hair combings, even the fabric of a chair on which their hero had sat. If their emotions were too intense, they even fainted," write Dorothy and Joseph Samachson in their book, *Masters of Music.*[2]

While this sounds like a description of how people acted at a Beatles concert, it isn't.

The Samachsons continue, "This was an audience of supposedly mature women in the sedate middle nineteenth century, and the man they were adoring was the most magnetic and popular pianist the concert stage had ever seen."[3]

His name was Franz Liszt. More than a century before the Beatles, he too inspired manic behavior. A German poet named Heinrich Heine took one look at the frenzied adulation that surrounded Liszt during a three-month stay in Berlin in 1841 and coined a name for it: Lisztomania.

As author Ronald Taylor observes, "The name of the King seemed to be not Friedrich Wilhelm IV von Hohenzollern but Franz Liszt. His portrait was displayed all over the city and cameos bearing his likeness were to be seen on the dresses of elegant ladies in salons and concert halls, where a rampant hero-worship raged, forerunner of the modern fan club and hysterical cult of the pop-star idol. . . . It needs only an irreverent flicker of the anachronistic imagination to picture 'I Love Franz' badges being proudly distributed among his female camp-followers, and even more proudly worn."[4]

This enthusiasm continued up to the moment of his departure from Berlin for the next stop on his performing tour. Even the king and queen drove out to watch him leave, though some members of the court grumbled that so much attention was being splashed on someone who wasn't of noble birth.

"A carriage pulled up, drawn by six white horses," wrote music critic Ludwig Rellstab. "Amid the shouting and cheering Liszt was practically carried down the steps and into the carriage, where he took his place beside the dignitaries of the university. Thirty coaches-and-four packed with students, and a number of riders on horseback, wearing their academic finery, accompanied his departure, and many other coaches also joined the cavalcade, while thousands swarmed around the scene on foot. Not only were the streets and squares crowded with people but all the windows along the way were filled with spectators."[5]

Similar spectacles occurred wherever Liszt performed. The only variation between one place and another lay in the degree of uncontrollability displayed by the ecstatic women in the audiences. Many would fight over the gloves that he took off and threw away before he started playing. Frequently the excitement extended even further.

"When he asked for a glass of water and put it down without draining it, the delirious beauties in the hall rushed forward at the end of the recital, picked up the glass and pressed it to their lips so as to quell their passion by taking a sip of the water he had left," Taylor says.[6]

Sometimes it seemed that nothing was too far-out to be claimed as a souvenir. Women often fought over his discarded cigar butts, and there's at least one case in which a woman emerged from one of these scrambles, lit it up her prize possession, and puffed away.

Besides the fact that Liszt and the Beatles each inspired a mania, there's another similarity: they also inspired movies. Eleven years after the release of *A Hard Day's Night*, director Ken Russell made a film called *Lisztomania* that was very loosely based on Liszt's life. In an unusual twist, Ringo Starr, the Beatles' drummer, plays the Pope in the Liszt movie.

The Beatles—Paul, George, Ringo and John—run down an alley with a mob of teenage girls not far behind. This is one of the opening scenes of their 1965 film, A Hard Day's Night. Director Richard Lester originally shot it in black and white, in a semi-documentary style that showed their activities during a single day. The movie concluded with a concert that showed the audience of mostly teenage girls screaming and crying. A Hard Day's Night is still popular today.

Liszt was fully conscious of the theatrical effect that he produced during his performances. In a letter he wrote to Lina Ramann, the author of his first biography, he compared his life to a play. Writing less than a year before his death, he said:

My insignificant career in performing and writing is divided up unclassically, like a Classic tragedy, into five acts:

1st = my childhood years until the death of my father, 1828;

2nd = 1830 to 1838, desultory studies and creativity in Paris and, for a time, in Geneva and Italy, before my reappearance in Vienna in 1838, the success of which launched me on my career as a virtuoso;

3rd = Concert tours: Paris, London, Berlin, Petersburg etc.: fantasias, transcriptions, *living like a lord;*

4th = 1848 to 1861, self-composure and work in Weimar;

5th = Its logical continuation and conclusion, in Rome, Budapest, Weimar from 1861 to . . .[7]

Yet despite the fame that would make his a household name, the story of Franz Liszt begins in obscurity. ◆

THE
LUDDITES

For generations, weavers in central English towns such as Nottingham had produced fine stockings and linen by hand. Many worked out of their homes. But in the early years of the 19th century, this long-established way of life changed with the invention of power looms, which were installed in large factories. Most weavers couldn't afford these new machines. They complained that the quality was inferior to what they could produce. At the same time, the English government adopted a policy by which the prices paid to these skilled weavers were no longer controlled. Prices fell, and the weavers made less money. Even worse, the price of wheat, which the workers purchased to make bread for their families, increased.

Angry workers banded together in protest. Early in 1811 they began breaking into factories and destroying machines. They soon acquired the name of Luddites because they claimed that they were acting under the orders of General Ned Ludd. According to one story, Ludd was an 18th-century worker who deliberately broke some machines. Another is that he was a mentally challenged person who accidentally damaged machines when he stumbled into them. There is some doubt as to whether Ludd was even a real person.

But there was no doubt about the effects of his "army." The actions of the Nottingham workers soon spread through the newly industrialized area that lay north of London. The government struck back. Laws were passed making machine breaking a crime that could be punished by death. Soldiers were summoned to the area, and some of the factory owners hired private guards. Many protesting workers were captured and some were executed.

In spite of these retaliatory efforts, the attacks continued. But it was a losing cause. Industrialization was a force that was too powerful to overcome. By 1816, the attacks ceased.

In recent years, however, the term *Luddites* has been revived as people become concerned about the social and economic effects of new technologies.

Composer Franz Joseph Haydn spent nearly 30 years of his life employed as music director for the aristocratic, music-loving Esterhazy family, the same people for whom Adam Liszt worked. Born in 1732, Haydn grew up as a choirboy before turning to composition. He was very prolific, writing 104 symphonies and hundreds of other works during his long career. He died in 1809.

Childhood Years

F ranz Liszt was born to Anna Maria and Adam Liszt in the tiny village of Doborján, now called Raiding in modern-day Hungary, on October 22, 1811. He would be the couple's only child.

Adam Liszt had learned how to play a number of musical instruments from his father. When he became a young man, he wanted to join the Franciscan Order, a group of Catholic friars. He was accepted as a novice but was asked to leave after two years. In order to earn a living, he entered the employ of the Esterhazys, the richest and most powerful family in Hungary. Eventually Adam got a job at Eisenstadt, where the family owned a large palace. He also played with the orchestra that the music-loving Esterhazy family maintained. There he met several important musicians, including famous composer Franz Joseph Haydn. In 1809 he was appointed to a position as administrator of the Esterhazys' sheep farms in Doborján. The job paid more money, but he could no longer play with the court orchestra. Soon after his arrival, he met Anna Maria Lager.

She had had a difficult life, as her father had died when she was eight and her mother died the following year. As a result, she was forced to begin working as a chambermaid in Vienna, the capital city of Austria. Then she moved in with her brother in a village close to Doborján. She was 22 when she met Adam, and he gave her the security she needed. They were married early in 1811.

At first, Franz was a somewhat sickly boy. When he was about two or three, his parents thought that he was about to die of small-pox and built a coffin for him. Fortunately they were wrong, though it took Franz several years to recover his strength. By this time he was becoming accustomed to hearing his father play a piano that had been installed in their house. When he was six, that piano would determine the future course of his life.

As his father recalled, "He heard me play a concerto by Ries in C-sharp minor. He leaned against the piano, listening, all ears. In the evening, when he came in from the garden where he had gone for a walk, he sang the theme of the concerto. We made him repeat it; he did not know what he was singing; that was the first indication we had of his genius. He kept on begging me to let him begin playing the piano with me."[1]

Adam was only too happy to oblige. Like many fathers, he may have felt frustrated at not being able to do what he really wanted to and hoped that his son would be more fortunate. He wrote in his journal, "My son, you are marked for destiny! You will achieve all the artistic hopes that fascinated me in vain as a youth. What was only a presentiment in me will in you be fulfilled. . . . In you I will again become young and will give forth."[2]

But there is no evidence that he pushed or mistreated his son to achieve this end. Franz, like other prodigies such as Wolfgang Amadeus Mozart, enjoyed practicing and made rapid progress. His father taught him music by all the most famous composers, from Johann Sebastian Bach to Ludwig van Beethoven, who was at the peak of his fame in Vienna.

His mother also had an important role in his upbringing. Later in life he said, "With reverence and tender affection I express my gratitude to my mother for the goodness and love that she invariably bore me. As a boy I was called a good son, but little of the credit for this belonged to me. How, indeed, could I have been other than a good son to so self-sacrificing a mother?"[3]

He played so much on the piano that he didn't have much time for schoolwork. As a grown man, he often commented that he could read music before he could read the alphabet.

He also showed early signs of the same religious impulse that had motivated his father. He became a Catholic and attended the local church regularly.

By the time Franz was eight, his father realized he was so far along in his development that he needed a professional teacher. Adam wanted to move to Vienna so that Franz could study with Carl Czerny, who had himself studied with Beethoven. He asked Prince Esterhazy for permission to move. The prince heard Franz play and was impressed. But at first he wouldn't allow the family to leave.

Adam was stubborn. If he couldn't get support from the prince, he would try elsewhere. In 1820 he arranged for Franz to play at two concerts in the nearby city of Oedenburg. Franz was sensational. Several Hungarian aristocrats pledged money.

Still, it took the family 18 months to finally make the move. They would leave behind a secure existence where they had a good home and plenty of food. It was very costly to live in Vienna. It would also put a lot of pressure on the narrow shoulders of a boy who wasn't even 10 years old.

The family soon gained the confidence they needed. Czerny had sent Adam a series of lessons to give his son, and Franz easily mastered them. Finally the prince gave Adam a leave of absence. He generously offered him his old job back if the experiment didn't work out.

The Liszts moved to Vienna in the spring of 1822, and Franz immediately began studying in person with Czerny. He also studied composition with Antonio Salieri, a famous composer. Both men were so impressed with their young student that they didn't charge anything for their time.

Soon Franz began giving private concerts. Then in December he gave his first public performance. Many more followed. According to one story, Beethoven attended one and kissed the young prodigy on the forehead.

After another concert, a newspaper wrote, "This handsome blond youth displayed such skill, lightness, accuracy, feeling and strength, such signs of mastery that the whole audience was delighted and astounded. Everyone was filled with the hope that,

Carl Czerny, who taught Liszt for several months, was himself a child prodigy. Born in 1791, he gave his first public performance as a pianist at the age of nine. He studied with Beethoven but soon realized that he was more interested in teaching and composing. He wrote hundreds of works, many of them as exercises for his students. He died in 1857.

through his splendid playing, he will bring honor to his father-land."[4]

With the image of Mozart, who had created a sensation at an even younger age, in front of him, Adam Liszt made a momentous decision. He resigned his post with Prince Esterhazy. His son's career was his top priority, and he had to begin a tour. They even followed much of the same route that Mozart had traveled more than half a century earlier. It didn't take long for Adam's decision to be justified. A paper in a German city early in the tour reported, "A new Mozart has appeared among us."[5]

Late in 1823 the family arrived in Paris. There they suffered a blow. Luigi Cherubini, the director of the Paris Conservatory of Music, wouldn't admit Franz to the school. The boy was a foreigner, said Cherubini, and the conservatory was only for French citizens. Since Cherubini was himself a foreigner, that seemed an odd position to take.

Luigi Cherubini was born in Florence, Italy in 1760 and had written several religious works by the time he was 13. When he was 28, he moved to Paris where he had success as a composer. In 1822, he became director of the Paris Conservatory and served in that position until his death 20 years later.

It was only a momentary setback. Franz's playing soon attracted rave reviews. He made two visits of several weeks to England, where he was well received, in 1824 and 1825. During both visits he played for King George IV.

Like Mozart, he was also spending much of his time composing. He composed an opera called *Don Sanche.* It premiered in Paris in 1825.

Two years later Franz and his father went to London for a third visit. But when they returned to France, tragedy struck. His father fell ill with typhoid fever and died.

Much later in his life, Franz recalled a prophetic deathbed conversation with Adam. He said his father "feared that women would trouble and dominate my life. This premonition was strong for, when sixteen years old, I had no idea of what a woman was."[6]

Author Derek Watkins sums up Adam's contribution. "Firm and ambitious, but never unkind or selfishly greedy, his hand had led Franz on a blazing path of success from an obscure corner of eastern Europe to the most cultivated capital cities. He had also instilled in him a religious reverence for his art which would never die. But now Liszt stood alone: he was not yet sixteen."[7]

My Country 'Tis of Thee

One of the most familiar patriotic songs in the United States is "America," which begins with the famous words *My country 'tis of thee/Sweet land of liberty*. It was composed by Samuel Francis Smith.

Samuel Francis Smith

Smith was born on October 21, 1808, in Boston, Massachusetts. He entered Harvard College just before his 17th birthday; he supported himself by serving as a translator and writing newspaper and magazine articles. After graduating in 1829, he began a career in journalism but quickly decided to become a minister. While he was studying at Andover Theological Academy in 1832, an organist friend named Lowell Mason asked him to translate some German songs into English. Smith became especially interested in one of them, "God Bless Our Native Land." He thought the United States needed a similar patriotic song, so he quickly wrote five verses. According to one story, it took him only half an hour. Because the fifth verse had some negative words toward the British, he soon cut it out.

The melody was already very popular. It was (and still is) used for the English anthem "God Save the Queen (or King)" and by more than a dozen other nations. In 1841, famous composer Ludwig van Beethoven wrote several piano variations on the same tune.

Smith's new song was performed for the first time on July 4, 1832, by a children's choir that Lowell Mason directed. It immediately became popular and quickly spread around the country. Though "The Star Spangled Banner" was adopted as our official national anthem in 1931, many people consider "America" to be our "unofficial" national anthem.

After graduating from theological school, Smith became a language teacher and pastor at a church near Boston. He married a woman whose last name was also Smith. In later life, he wrote more than 150 church hymns, edited a missionary magazine, and became the secretary of the Baptist Missionary Union, traveling around the United States and to many foreign countries. When he died on November 16, 1895, his funeral ceremonies included the singing of "America."

Franz Liszt as a young man. Considered by many people to be the greatest pianist who ever lived, Liszt believed that his physical appearance matched his talent. He was careful about the way he dressed. When he performed in public, he often pinned medals on his chest and wore a sword that was decorated with many jewels.

CHAPTER **3**

Desultory Studies and Creativity

His father's death caused Franz to take a closer look at his life. He was starting to realize that no matter how well he played, because he had not been born to the aristocracy, he would be considered as little better than a servant.

"I developed a bitter aversion to art as I saw it: more or less debased to the level of trade for profit, labeled as a source of amusement for fashionable society. I would rather have done anything else in the world than be a musician in the service of a great lord, patronized and paid like a juggler or performing dog."[1]

He stopped performing and began reading a great deal, trying to make up for all the years he'd spent practicing the piano and touring. He also gave piano lessons to support his mother and himself. It didn't take him long to fall in love with Caroline de Saint-Cricq, one of his pupils. She felt the same way about him and they began spending hours together after the lessons. Caroline's mother encouraged their romance. Unfortunately, Caroline's father didn't. He was a government official who believed that he and his family were far superior to the young musician. Even though Caroline's mother begged him to let the couple stay together, he refused to allow Franz even to enter the house. He quickly ordered his daughter to marry a wealthy landowner.

That incident only reinforced Liszt's awareness of his own humble origins. He fell into a depression that lasted two years. He became ill, and rumors of his death began to circulate. A French newspaper called *Le Corsaire* carried his obituary in its October 23, 1828, edition. Some shop windows in Paris even carried his picture with the legend "born 22 October 1811, died in Paris 1828."

He wasn't dead. In fact, he tried to become a priest, but his mother and his confessor opposed such a move. Not surprisingly, he didn't compose very much music. He lived in seclusion with his mother.

Events outside his control eventually snapped him out of his depression. The July Revolution in Paris—a brief popular uprising in 1830—drove out King Charles X and replaced him with King Louis-Philippe. The new king was considered to be in favor of democratic reforms.

The results of the uprising led to a sudden surge in feelings of liberty. Liszt broke out of his composing doldrums. "It was the cannon that cured him," his mother often said afterward.[2] He quickly became acquainted with many of the important artistic and musical figures in Paris, the cultural hub of France. One person was painter Eugène Delacroix, whose *Liberty Leading the People* summed up the popular feelings. In this famous painting, a determined-looking woman who represents freedom carries a French flag in her right hand and a rifle with a bayonet in her left. She is at the head of a large group of equally determined-looking armed men. They are steadily advancing, and Delacroix wanted his viewers to believe that they will win.

Another friend was composer Hector Berlioz, who was eight years older than Liszt and helped expand the limits of his imagination. Berlioz composed on a grand scale. In 1830, his *Symphonie Fantastique* premiered and Liszt was in the audience. Liszt was so

Composer Frédéric Chopin, who was born in Poland in 1810, spent much of his life in France. He died of tuberculosis when he was only 39.

impressed with the music that he decided to make a piano transcription of the work. This was the first of his many transcriptions, which are rearrangements of original compositions so that they can be played by different types of instruments.

A third was Frédéric Chopin, another pianist. Chopin had grown up in Poland but was living in Paris. The two young men became close friends, even though their styles of piano playing were entirely different. Liszt was flashy and flamboyant, while Chopin's playing was much more muted.

But the most important influence during Liszt's artistic rebirth was attending an 1831 concert by virtuoso violinist Niccolo Paganini. Ronald Taylor writes, "[Liszt] never recovered from the experience. . . . Paganini's sheer technical wizardry, Paganini the musical acrobat, took Liszt's breath away and fired him to make himself, both as composer and performer, the Paganini of the keyboard."[3]

Part of the secret was practice, practice, and still more practice to acquire a flawless technique. Liszt spent four or five hours every day at his piano, trying to match Paganini's skill level. The other part was showmanship. Liszt already had an outgoing musical personality. All he needed to do was exaggerate his mannerisms.

That same year he began living up to his father's prophecy. The young man who said he had no idea of what a woman was four years earlier was quickly finding out. He became involved with several women and spent a few months in 1832 with one of them at her remote home in the Swiss Alps.

Early in 1833 he met another woman, the Countess Marie d'Agoult. She was nearly six years older than Liszt. She was also a noblewoman who was married with two children. It didn't matter to the couple. For one thing, her marriage had been arranged by her mother and Marie felt no love for her husband, who was 15 years older than she was. However, it was important to keep up appearances, so Franz and Marie could meet only in secret. When one of her daughters died late in 1834, she went into seclusion.

By spring the following year she had recovered and began seeing Liszt again. Soon she found that she was pregnant. It would have been almost impossible for them to live together in Paris because of the scandal that that would cause. They decided to go to Swit-

Listening to a concert presented by violinist Niccolo Paganini (left) had a great influence on Franz Liszt. Painter Eugene Delacroix (right) became a good friend.

zerland. They settled in Geneva, where Liszt taught at the conservatory of music and composed. Marie became a writer; she would publish several books under the name of Daniel Stern. Late that year their daughter Blandine was born.

But Liszt wasn't completely happy. He had heard about another performer named Sigismond Thalberg who had become the most famous pianist in Paris. Liszt wanted to challenge him to a duel—not with guns or swords, but with pianos. He and Marie traveled back to Paris in the autumn of 1836. Thalberg was gone on a lengthy concert tour, so Liszt had to wait until the following spring. They met on March 31, 1837, and Liszt easily defeated his opponent.

He and Marie soon left Paris and traveled to Italy, where they rented a house on the shores of Lake Como. They spent most of their time together, reading classics such as Dante's *Divine Comedy* and going for long walks. On Christmas Eve that year, they had another daughter, whom they named Cosima after Lake Como. For Marie, her happiness was complete. She believed that Liszt felt the same way.

She was wrong. He soon became bored with living so quietly. He missed being in front of adoring audiences. Within a few months after Cosima's birth, it was evident that he wanted to return. Soon he had the perfect excuse to resume his exciting lifestyle.

Early in 1838, a severe flood damaged parts of Hungary. Though he hadn't been back to his native land for many years, he said that it was his duty to help out his countrymen. The best way to do that, he believed, was to give benefit concerts. The best place to give them was in Vienna, the capital of the huge empire that included Hungary and was even more important than Paris as a center of European music.

As a foreigner with a scandalous reputation, Liszt was investigated by the chief of police. The chief decided that Liszt didn't pose any danger, and he closed his report with the following comment: "He appears to me simply as a vain and frivolous young man who affects the eccentric manners of the young Frenchmen of the day, but good-natured and, apart from his merits as an artist, of no significance."[4]

He couldn't have been more mistaken. Lisztomania was about to sweep across Europe. ◆

Remember the Alamo!

Santa Anna

By 1821, very few Mexicans were living in their country's province of Texas, which lay north of the Rio Grande. The Mexican government decided to populate the area by encouraging foreign immigration, offering large tracts of land and tax advantages to anyone who would settle there. Thousands of residents of the new United States swarmed southwest. Many empty cabins had the words *Gone to Texas* scrawled on their doors.

Soon the new arrivals far outnumbered the original Mexican population, and they set up their own government. It didn't take long for the settlers to come into conflict with the Mexican government, which was under the leadership of Antonio López de Santa Anna. He decided it was time to teach the Texans a brutal lesson.

Late in 1835, Santa Anna marched north with an army of more than 2,000 soldiers. During his advance, about 200 Texans—including such famous historical figures as Davy Crockett, William Travis, and James Bowie— barricaded themselves inside the Alamo, an old mission in modern-day San Antonio. They hoped that they would receive enough reinforcements to hold off Santa Anna's troops. They didn't. Santa Anna arrived in late February and began shelling the Alamo. Then he stormed the mission early in the morning of March 6, 1836. Although the defenders continually gunned down Mexican soldiers, the Mexican troops managed to punch holes in the mission walls and pour inside. All the defenders were killed. Two weeks later, another group of nearly 400 Texans surrendered to Santa Anna at the town of Goliad. Acting under his orders, Santa Anna's troops executed nearly all of their prisoners.

"Remember the Alamo!" and "Remember Goliad!" became rallying cries for Texans. Under the command of Sam Houston, a band of Texans defeated Santa Anna's army at the Battle of San Jacinto on April 21. Santa Anna was captured. Texas won independence from Mexico. It became the 28th state in the United States on December 29, 1845.

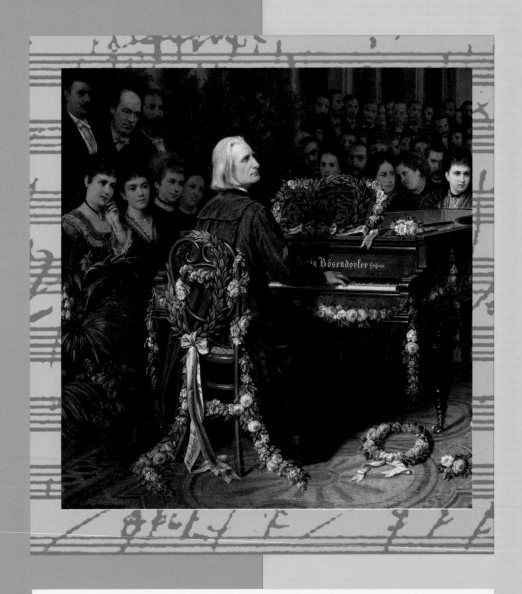

Franz Liszt performs a recital sometime after taking Holy Orders during the 1860s. His audience listens attentively and respectfully. Their calm demeanor is very different from the enthusiasm and adulation with which his concerts were received during his eight-year tour when he was a younger man.

CHAPTER

4

Living Like a Lord

F ranz Liszt returned to Italy and spent several months with Marie. In May 1839 the couple's third child, a son named Daniel, was born. But Liszt quickly found another excuse to leave Marie and his children. Plans were being made to put up a statue of Beethoven in his native city of Bonn, Germany. Liszt went back to Vienna for another series of concerts to help raise money for the statue. Marie took the children and returned to Paris. Although they would see each other from time to time during the next few years, their relationship was essentially over. Liszt's concert career was about to shift into high gear.

To heighten the effect of his playing, he turned the piano sideways. Before that, pianists had either directly faced the audience or played with their backs to their listeners. Liszt was aware that he was a handsome man who looked especially good in profile. He would sit down, turn toward the audience until they quieted down, then begin to play. Some notes could barely be heard. At other times he would pound the keys so hard that the strings broke.

Even more innovative, he decided that he would do an entirely different kind of concert. Up to that time, it was common practice for several individual artists to share playing time, often with an orchestra. But Liszt decided that he would go it alone. Because he had committed the works he would play to memory, he didn't even need someone to turn the pages of the musical scores. There would be nothing to distract the audiences from him.

At first he termed what he was doing a "musical soliloquy." Soon it became known as a "recital." When he staged his first long tour, in England in 1840–1841, his new concert style was greeted with some snickering. "What does he mean? How can one *recite* upon the piano?" was a typical comment.

Audiences soon found out. In the decade since he'd heard Paganini, Liszt had honed his effects to the hilt. He'd select attention-getting music, often his own. As he entered the stage, decorations would clank against his chest and a jeweled sword he'd been awarded during a visit to Hungary in 1840 would swing by his side. He'd survey the audience, his shoulder-length hair tossing as he turned from side to side.

Russian music critic Vladimir Stasov described what would happen next:

He tore off his white kid gloves and tossed them on the floor, under the piano. Then, after bowing low in all directions to a tumult of applause such as had probably not been heard in Petersburg since 1703, he seated himself at the piano. Instantly the hall became deadly silent. Without any preliminaries, Liszt began playing the opening cello phrase of the *William Tell Overture.* As soon as he finished, and while the hall was still rocking with applause, he moved swiftly to a second piano facing in the opposite direction. . . We had never in our lives heard anything like this; we had never been in the presence of such a brilliant, passionate, demonic temperament, at one moment rushing like a whirlwind, at another pouring forth cascades of tender beauty and grace.[1]

Richard Wagner (pronounced REE-kard VAHG-ner), who would became world-famous many years later as an operatic composer, attended a recital. He was very impressed. "Entering the crowded hall," he wrote, "I saw that the platform on which the grand piano stood was under intense siege from the pick of Parisian female society. I witnessed the enthusiastic ovations accorded to the revered, world-famed virtuoso, listened to a number of his bravura pieces . . . and came away in a helpless daze."[2]

Liszt knew that he was in complete control, and he wasn't shy about letting people, even royalty, know. During one trip to Russia, he gave a private recital for Czar Nicholas I and the members of his court. At one point, the czar began a conversation. Liszt quickly stopped playing. The czar was stunned. He asked Liszt if there was a problem.

As Taylor writes, "'When the Emperor [Liszt himself] speaks,' answered Liszt calmly, 'all others must be silent.' The [czar] was somewhat taken aback, and Liszt continued his recital in the reverential silence which both he and the music demanded."[3]

During the eight years that he crisscrossed Europe in what he called his *glanzperiode* ("time of glitter"), his lifestyle would have been familiar to modern rock stars. In addition to the adulation of his fans—sometimes his concerts attracted more than 3,000 people—he stayed in fancy hotels, enjoyed fine food, and wore expensive clothing. It was a far cry from the dismal days not much more than a decade earlier when he felt like he was on the level of a performing dog.

But there was one big difference between him and modern rock musicians: transportation. Liszt lived in a time when there were no jet airplanes, luxurious buses, or limousines. He traveled great distances in uncomfortable carriages with primitive suspension systems. Most of the roads at that time were dirt, and he must have felt every pothole and rock that the carriages bounced over. Carriages were unheated, and much of his traveling took place during cold weather. Sometimes he didn't even have the protection of a covered carriage, crossing windswept, snowy landscapes in open sleighs. During one trip to England, he traveled 2,200 miles in 67 days, giving 45 concerts in 31 different cities and towns.

Despite the rigors of all his traveling, he still maintained his human feeling. While on tour in southern France in 1844, he met up with Caroline de Saint-Cricq, whose father had broken off their relationship when they were teenagers and forced her to marry someone else. That marriage had proven to be an unhappy one. "I love you still with every ounce of my soul, and I want you to enjoy a happiness which I myself no longer know," she wrote.[4]

In return, Liszt sent her a bracelet that contained a valuable turquoise and composed a beautiful song of farewell to her. He even bequeathed her a ring in the will that he wrote in 1860, but she never got it—she died before he did.

After a few more years of touring, Liszt was beginning to think it might be time to settle down and concentrate on composing. He felt that he needed two things in order to be successful: a great deal of money, and female companionship. It didn't take him long to find them.

Early in 1847 he gave a series of concerts in Russia, many in the city of Kiev. There he met Princess Carolyne Sayn-Wittgenstein. She owned a huge estate called Woronice, not far from Kiev, and she was separated from her husband. She invited Liszt to stay with her. While she was not very attractive physically and smoked cigars, she was extremely cultured and adored him. He continued to tour for several more months, gave what would be his final paid recital in October, then returned to Woronice to spend the fall and winter with Carolyne.

His career as a concert pianist was over. A new career was about to begin. ◆

THE IRISH POTATO FAMINE

In the late summer of 1845, a terrible disaster struck Ireland. Most of the potatoes that were harvested quickly turned black and slimy. The cause was a type of fungus.

At that time, Ireland was under the control of England. A high percentage of the Irish population lived on small farms that they rented from English landlords, many of whom lived hundreds of miles away. Most of the farms contained fewer than fifteen acres, and many didn't even have five. Nearly all of these farms grew no other crops beside potatoes. That was the only food that could be produced in big enough quantities to feed large families on such small acreages.

Searching for potatoes during the Irish potato famine

With the blight, there were no more potatoes to eat. Within a few months thousands of people had starved to death. A few people forced themselves to eat the disgusting tubers. They soon contracted contagious diseases, which killed even more people. Because they couldn't pay the rent to their landlords, many people were forced to leave their farms. They were packed together in workhouses, which became breeding grounds for disease.

For many Irish, the only alternative was to flee. Thousands of families somehow scraped together enough money to board ships that would carry them to Canada and the United States. But these ships had their own set of horrors. They acquired the name of "coffin ships" because hundreds died from being cramped together in unsanitary conditions during the weeks it took to cross the storm-tossed Atlantic Ocean.

The famine finally ended in 1850. No one knows how many people died, though estimates range between 500,000 and one million. Probably at least another million emigrated. In terms of population, Ireland has never recovered from the catastrophe. When the potato famine struck, the country had an estimated population of more than eight million people. Even today the population is only about five and a half million.

Franz Liszt was one of the most generous people in the history of music. After retiring from his long concert-touring career in 1847, he never again charged money to perform in public. He also gave encouragement and advice to many musicians. One time a young pianist falsely advertised that she had been his pupil. She apologized to Liszt, who asked her to play for a few minutes. He offered a few suggestions and told her that now she could honestly say she had been his pupil.

Chapter 5

Self-Composure and Work

I n 1842, Liszt had been appointed Grand Ducal Director of Music Extraordinaire at the court of Weimar, a small kingdom in central Germany. Back then, he was much too busy touring to be able to spend much time there. Once he retired from the concert circuit, he could finally take advantage of this appointment. At Weimar, he would have an entire orchestra at his disposal. He could spend his time composing, conducting, and producing concerts.

One of his goals at Weimar was to create new musical forms. The most important of these was the symphonic poem. Also known as program music, this form is a composition based on other kinds of art, such as a picture, a landscape, or a literary work. It tells a story or sets a scene through music. Liszt would eventually create 13 of them and inspire other composers to write many more.

By 1847 his influence was so strong that many musicians flocked to Weimar to spend time with him. He generously gave piano lessons and promoted the works of other composers. One of these was Richard Wagner. Though Wagner was only two years younger than Liszt, he was not very well known. Liszt was instrumental in producing Wagner's opera *Lohengrin*. Wagner wasn't around to see it. He left Weimar soon after his arrival because he was threatened with arrest for his political activities. Later he would become one of the most important people in Liszt's life.

Personally, Liszt lived comfortably. He and Carolyne had servants to wait on them. They would often give elaborate, expensive parties that included delicacies such as oysters, truffles, and champagne.

With everything going so well, it isn't surprising that this was a very fertile time for his composing. In addition to symphonic poems such as *Les Préludes* and *Mazeppa,* he also composed longer pieces such as *Dante Symphony, A Faust Symphony, Dance of Death (Totentanz) for Piano and Orchestra,* and a great deal of other work.

The good times wouldn't last forever. Many people disapproved of his lifestyle. Carolyne often had to leave Weimar to escape hostile glances and gossip. The worst blow came when the czar of Russia wouldn't sanction her divorce.

Not everyone liked Liszt's music. The young composer Johannes Brahms met him in 1853. Even though Liszt could and would have helped him, Brahms was very opposed to Liszt's musical style. Liszt was a Romantic, which meant that he believed in portraying strong emotion in his music. Brahms believed in the older classical forms. He also didn't approve of Liszt's efforts to create new types of compositions. Brahms even fell asleep during one of Liszt's recitals.

The duke who had given Liszt his appointment died in 1853, and his successor didn't care as much for music. Finally, some of the music Liszt presented was booed by audiences. He resigned his post in Weimar at the end of 1858, though he stayed there well over two more years.

The fourth act of his life had come to an end.◆

FRANZ Kafka

Frank Kafka, one of the most famous writers of the early 20th century, was born in Prague (in modern-day Czech Republic) in 1883. At the time of his birth, Prague was part of the Austria-Hungarian Empire. As he was growing up, Kafka often came into conflict with his father, who disapproved of nearly everything that his son did and left him with very little self-confidence.

Kafka began writing when he was 16 but soon destroyed all his early works. He studied law and obtained his degree in 1906. He took a job with an insurance company and continued to live at home, where he often wrote at nights.

Nearly all his stories and novels have bizarre plots and involve individuals who are caught in nightmarish situations that they can't control. They reflected Kafka's belief that most people are powerless in modern society. One of his first works was a short story called "The Metamorphosis." It begins with a very well-known line: "As Gregor Samsa awoke one morning from uneasy dreams he found himself transformed in his bed into a gigantic insect." The insect is a cockroach, and Gregor dies when his father throws an apple core at him. In his novel *The Trial*, the narrator is accused of crimes about which he knows nothing by people he can't see or meet. He becomes increasingly frustrated as he makes many unsuccessful attempts to obtain justice and prove that he isn't guilty. Finally he is stabbed to death.

Franz Kafka died of tuberculosis in 1924. During his life he published only a few stories, though he had written many more. One of his last wishes was that everything he had produced be destroyed. His friend Max Brod did not honor that wish. Instead, he edited Kafka's works and had them published, insuring that Kafka's reputation as an original writer would survive. Many of his works are considered classics of modern fiction.

Franz Liszt shares a moment with composer Richard Wagner and Wagner's wife Cosima. Cosima was also Liszt's daughter. She was originally married to Hans von Bülow, a famous conductor. Then she fell in love with Wagner. Liszt didn't approve. He was even unhappier when Wagner insisted that Cosima abandon the Catholic faith and become a Protestant to marry him. For several years, Liszt refused to speak to them. But eventually they were reconciled.

Continuation and Conclusion

A fter resigning his position at Weimar, Liszt soon began
a pattern that would last for the rest of his life. He
alternated between living in Rome, in Budapest, and
back at Weimar.

Rome was the first stop. He arrived there in October 1861 after
making a brief visit to Marie d'Agoult. It was the last time they
would see each other.

Meanwhile, Princess Carolyne had been in Rome for nearly a
year and a half, trying to get her marriage annulled so that she and
Franz could be wed. She had apparently succeeded, and many
people believe that if the couple had moved a little more quickly
they could have become man and wife. But for some reason they
hesitated. It is quite likely that Liszt really didn't want to be married. Eventually the Pope was persuaded to withdraw his blessing
by members of her ex-husband's family.

Then in 1865, Liszt made a decision that removed the possibility
of his marrying Carolyne or anyone else. He took Holy Orders in
the Catholic Church and became known as Abbé Liszt. Though he
couldn't hear confessions or celebrate a mass, he often wore the
black cassock of a priest and lived for a while in Vatican City, not

far from the Pope. While he and Carolyne remained on friendly terms, she had less and less influence over him as the years went on.

By that time, he had suffered the deaths of two of his three children. Daniel died in 1959 and Blandine followed three years later. Liszt became close to his only surviving child, Cosima. She had married a pianist and conductor named Hans von Bülow in 1857.

It came as a severe blow when Liszt realized that Cosima was romantically involved with Richard Wagner, whose musical reputation had increased since their early meeting at Weimar. Liszt was very close to both men, but strongly disapproved of breaking up the marriage. After having three children with Wagner, Cosima finally divorced von Bülow and married Wagner in 1870. Liszt was shocked. He broke off relations with them for several years, but eventually, they reconciled.

For the rest of his life, Liszt was the Grand Old Man of Music in Europe. Virtually every composer visited him at some point.

In 1886 he made a final concert tour, which included playing in front of Queen Victoria. On the way back, he stopped to visit Cosima in Bayreuth. Wagner had died three years earlier, but festivals of his music were staged there annually. During his visit, Liszt fell ill with pneumonia and died shortly before midnight on July 31. He was buried in Bayreuth, next to Wagner. Cosima joined them decades later, in 1930.

While he was the first superstar piano virtuoso, most historians rank a number of other composers above him. But in terms of his breadth of accomplishment and his influence, few can compare. In addition to composing and playing the piano, he was a conductor, a music critic, a transcriber, a teacher, and a concert promoter. It would be hard to find another musician who was as generous with his time and his interest in advancing the careers of others. By the end of his life he had become an icon. ◆

Lady Liberty

The Statue of Liberty was born at a dinner party in Paris, France, in 1865. A 31-year-old sculptor named Frédéric-Auguste Bartholdi and several friends wanted their country to give the United States a present in 1876, the centennial of the Declaration of Independence.

Political problems inside France and a war with Germany delayed the project. It wasn't until 1874 that it got under way. Bartholdi designed the statue with help from Alexandre-Gustave Eiffel, who would later build the Eiffel Tower, one of the most famous landmarks in Paris.

Everything about the statue was massive. It stretched 152 feet from toe to torch tip. Even the nose was four and a half feet long. It was very expensive. Eventually it was decided that France would pay for the statue itself, while the United States would pay for the base and its installation. However, it still proved very difficult to raise the money. There was no chance of even starting by the 1876 anniversary. Construction began in 1881 and was completed three years later.

During this time, almost nothing had been done in the United States. Many people were outraged that the base would cost as much as the statue. Others believed that New York City, where the statue would be located, should pay the entire cost. Then newspaper publisher Joseph Pulitzer stepped in. He publicly criticized the wealthy for not stepping up. He also promised to print the names of all contributors in his newspaper, even if they only gave a penny. That did the trick. Pulitzer exceeded his fund-raising goal, and the base was constructed on Ellis Island in New York Harbor.

In France, the statue was taken apart into 350 individual pieces, loaded onto a ship, and carried across the Atlantic in 1885. After being reassembled and installed on the base, it was finally dedicated on October 28, 1886, with U.S. president Grover Cleveland presiding over the ceremonies. Ever since then, the Statue of Liberty has been one of this country's most enduring symbols of freedom.

Selected Works

Orchestral Works
A Faust Symphony
Dante Symphony
Piano Concerto #1
Piano Concerto #2
Dance of Death (Totentanz) for Piano
    and Orchestra

Piano Works
Sonata in B Minor
Transcendental Études
Hungarian Rhapsodies
Liebesträume ("Love's Dream")
Mephisto Waltz
Rhapsodie Espagnole

Symphonic Poems
Les Préludes
Mazeppa
Tasso
Hamlet
Orpheus
Prometheus

Choral Music
Saint Elisabeth Oratorio
Christus Oratorio
Missa Choralis

Chronology

1811	Born on October 22
1820	Gives first concert
1822	Family moves to Vienna, Austria; begins studying with Czerny and Salieri
1823	Family moves to Paris, France
1824	Plays first concert for King George IV of England
1825	His opera *Don Sanche* premieres in Paris
1827	Father dies; Franz deeply affected for many months
1829	Loses interest in music
1831	Attends concert by virtuoso violinist Niccolo Paganini and is reinspired
1833	Meets Countess Marie d'Agoult
1835	Elopes to Switzerland with Marie; birth of daughter Blandine
1837	Birth of daughter Cosima at Lake Como, Italy
1838	Gives benefit performance in Vienna, which leads to extensive touring
1839	Son Daniel is born
1842	Is appointed Grand Ducal Director of Music Extraordinaire at the court of Weimar
1844	Breaks off relationship with Marie d'Agoult
1847	Meets Princess Carolyne Sayn-Wittgenstein; ends virtuoso career
1848	Settles in Weimar in post of music director
1858	Resigns post in Weimar
1859	Death of son Daniel
1862	Daughter Blandine dies in childbirth
1863	Enters monastery in Rome
1865	Enters Vatican, receives tonsure and minor orders
1866	Mother dies
1870	Daughter Cosima marries Richard Wagner
1886	Dies of pneumonia on July 31

1770	Composer Ludwig van Beethoven is born.
1782	Composer and virtuoso violinist Niccolo Paganini is born.
1789	The French Revolution begins.
1803	Composer Hector Berlioz is born.
1810	Composer Frédéric Chopin is born.
1811	Luddite Revolts in England begin.
1813	Composers Richard Wagner and Giuseppe Verdi are born.
1814	Francis Scott Key writes the words to "The Star Spangled Banner."
1826	French artist Joseph-Nicéphore Niepce takes world's first photograph, which requires an eight-hour exposure.
1827	Composer Ludwig van Beethoven dies.
1829	George Stephenson develops famous "Rocket" locomotive, which stimulates railroad development.
1831	Victor Hugo writes *The Hunchback of Notre Dame.*
1833	Composer Johannes Brahms is born.
1836	The Battle of the Alamo is fought in Texas.
1837	Samuel Morse invents the telegraph.
1845	Edgar Allan Poe writes poem "The Raven."
1861	The U.S. Civil War begins.
1863	Henry Ford, who founds Ford Motor Company, is born.
1865	U.S. Civil War ends; President Abraham Lincoln is assassinated.
1869	The Suez Canal opens, joining the Mediterranean and Red Seas.
1870	French author Jules Verne publishes *20,000 Leagues Under the Sea.*
1875	Georges Bizet composes *Carmen,* perhaps the world's most popular opera.
1876	U.S. author Mark Twain publishes *The Adventures of Tom Sawyer.*
1877	Thomas Edison invents the phonograph.
1883	Richard Wagner dies; future Italian dictator Benito Mussolini is born.
1886	The Statue of Liberty is dedicated in New York Harbor.
1889	Future German dictator Adolf Hitler is born; the Eiffel Tower is built in Paris.
1919	After being defeated in World War I, the Germans draw up a new constitution in Weimar, the same town where Liszt lived for over a decade.
1930	Liszt's daughter Cosima Wagner dies.

Chapter Notes

Chapter 1   Lisztomania

1. Sandy Gardiner, "Heavy Disc Dose Spreads Disease in England," *The Ottawa Journal,* November 9, 1963 (http://beatles.ncf.ca/sandyg.html, n.d.).

2. Dorothy Samachson and Joseph Samachson, *Masters of Music* (New York: Doubleday & Company, 1967), p. 148.

3. Ibid.

4. Ronald Taylor, *Liszt: The Man and the Musician* (London: Grafton Books, 1986), p. 79.

5. Ibid., p. 80.

6. Ibid., p. 86.

7. Ernst Burger, *Franz Liszt: A Chronicle of His Time in Pictures and Documents,* translated by Stewart Spencer (Princeton, N.J.: Princeton University Press, 1989), p. 5.

Chapter 2   Childhood Years

1. Ernst Burger, *Franz Liszt: A Chronicle of His Time in Pictures and Documents,* translated by Stewart Spencer (Princeton, N.J.: Princeton University Press, 1989), p. 12.

2. Derek Watson, *The Master Musicians: Liszt* (London: J.M. Dent & Sons, Ltd., 1989), p. 8.

3. Ronald Taylor, *Liszt: The Man and the Musician* (London: Grafton Books, 1986), p. 4.

4. Watson, p. 14.

5. Ibid., p. 15.

6. Ibid., p. 21.

7. Ibid.

Chapter 3   Desultory Studies and Creativity

1. Ernst Burger, *Franz Liszt: A Chronicle of His Time in Pictures and Documents,* translated by Stewart Spencer (Princeton, N.J.: Princeton University Press, 1989), p. 56.

2. Ibid., p. 63.

3. Ronald Taylor, *Liszt: The Man and the Musician* (London: Grafton Books, 1986), p. 25.

4. Victor Seroff, *Franz Liszt: An Illustrated Biography* (New York: The MacMillan Company, 1966), p. 56.

Chapter 4   Living Like a Lord

1. Ernst Burger, *Franz Liszt: A Chronicle of His Time in Pictures and Documents,* translated by Stewart Spencer (Princeton, N.J.: Princeton University Press, 1989), p. 141.

2. Ronald Taylor, *Liszt: The Man and the Musician* (London: Grafton Books, 1986), pp. 76–77.

3. Ibid., p. 83.

4. Burger, p. 54.

For Further Reading

For Young Adults

Getzinger, Donna, and Daniel Felsenfeld. *Richard Wagner and German Opera*. Greensboro, N.C.: Morgan Reynolds Publishing, 2004.

Jacobson, Julius. *The Classical Music Experience*. Naperville, Ill.: Sourcebooks, Inc., 2003.

Vernon, Roland. *Introducing Chopin*. Parsippany, N.J.: Silver Burdett Press, 1996.

Internet Addresses

Biographies: Franz Joseph Liszt
http://www.maurice-abravanel.com/liszt_franz_english.html

Franz Liszt—Commentary & Biography
http://www.d-vista.com/OTHER/franzliszt2.html

Franz Liszt—Timeline
http://www.d-vista.com/OTHER/Lizsttime.html
http://www.d-vista.com/OTHER/Lizsttime2.html

Ottawa Beatles Site
http://beatles.ncf.ca/sandyg.html. n.d.

Luddites
http://www.spartacus.schoolnet.co.uk/PRluddites.htm
http://carbon.cudenver.edu/~mryder/itc_data/luddite.html
http://www.bigeastern.com/ludd/nl_whats.htm

My Country 'Tis of Thee
http://www.sbgmusic.com/html/teacher/reference/composers/smith.html
http://www.miketodd.net/encyc/americasong.htm

Remember the Alamo!
http://www.tsha.utexas.edu/handbook/online/articles/view/AA/qea2.html
http://hotx.com/alamo/background.html

The Irish Potato Famine
http://www.wikipedia.org/wiki/Irish_potato_famine
http://www.digitalhistory.uh.edu/historyonline/irish_potato_famine.cfm
http://www.people.virginia.edu/~eas5e/Irish/Famine.html

Franz Kafka
http://www.kafka-franz.com/kafka-Biography.htm
http://www.tameri.com/csw/exist/kafka.asp

Lady Liberty
http://www.greatbuildings.com/buildings/Statue_of_Liberty.html
http://www.americanparknetwork.com/parkinfo/sl/history/liberty.html

Works Consulted

Burger, Ernst. *Franz Liszt: A Chronicle of His Time in Pictures and Documents*. Translated by Stewart Spencer. Princeton, N.J.: Princeton University Press, 1989.

Goulding, Phil G. *Classical Music: The 50 Greatest Composers and Their 1,000 Greatest Works*. New York: Ballantine Books, 1992.

Samachson, Dorothy, and Joseph Samachson. *Masters of Music*. New York: Doubleday & Company, 1967.

Schonberg, Harold. *The Lives of the Great Composers*. New York: W.W. Norton, 1981.

Seroff, Victor. *Franz Liszt: An Illustrated Biography*. New York: The MacMillan Company, 1966.

Taylor, Ronald. *Liszt: The Man and the Musician*. London: Grafton Books, 1986.

Watson, Derek. *The Master Musicians: Liszt*. London: J.M. Dent & Sons, Ltd., 1989.

Index